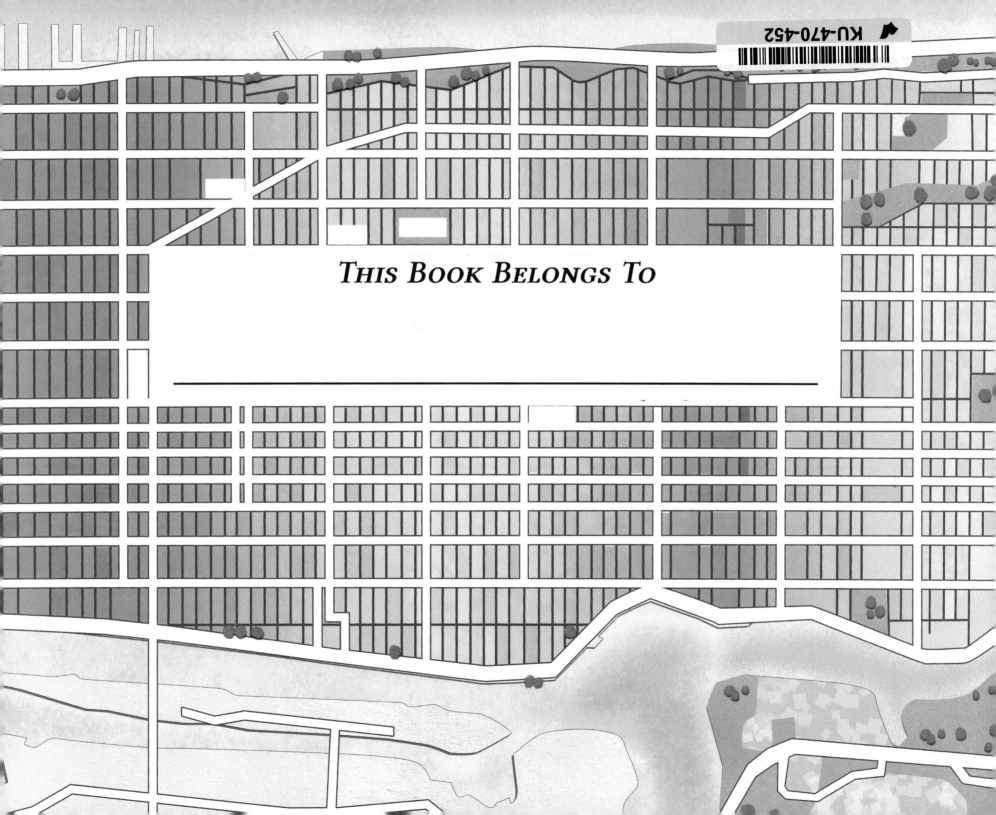

THIS BOOK BELONGS TO

_____

Neue Galerie

Ukrainian Institute

Cooper Hewitt

Frick Collection

Guggenheim

Met Museum

Jewish Museum

**American Museum
of Natural History**

**New York Historical
Society**

MAD Museum

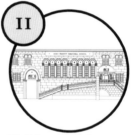

**Children's Museum
of Manhattan**

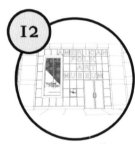

**American Folk Art
Museum**

**Museum at
Eldridge Street**

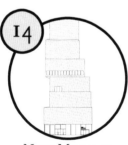

New Museum

Intrepid Museum

Fireman's Museum

**Museum of the
American Indian**

Whitney Museum

COLOR
NYC MUSEUMS

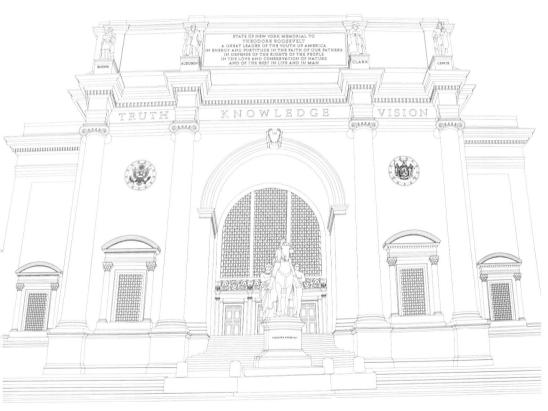

STATE OF NEW YORK MEMORIAL TO
THEODORE ROOSEVELT
A GREAT LEADER OF THE YOUTH OF AMERICA
IN ENERGY AND FORTITUDE IN THE FAITH OF OUR FATHERS
IN DEFENSE OF THE RIGHTS OF THE PEOPLE
IN THE LOVE AND CONSERVATION OF NATURE
AND OF THE BEST IN LIFE AND IN MAN

TRUTH   KNOWLEDGE   VISION

BY
JAKE ROSE

Color Our Town Publishers
74 E 79 Street
New York, NY 10075
www.colorourtown.com

ISBN 978-1-948286-02-2

Printed in USA

Cover and back cover designed by D. J. Hacker and Agnieszka Koscisz.
Line illustrations by Ashmita Nandi, Claudio Icuza, Ivan Myerchuk, and Kajal Saini.

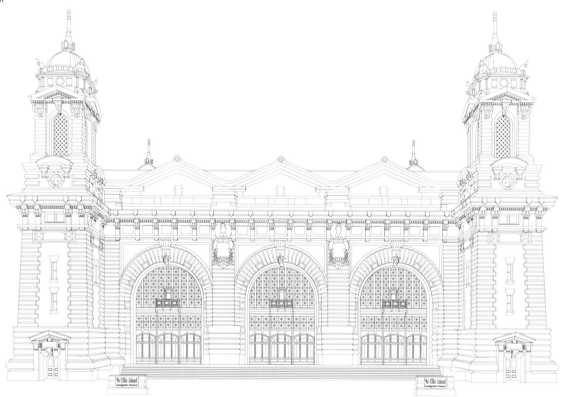

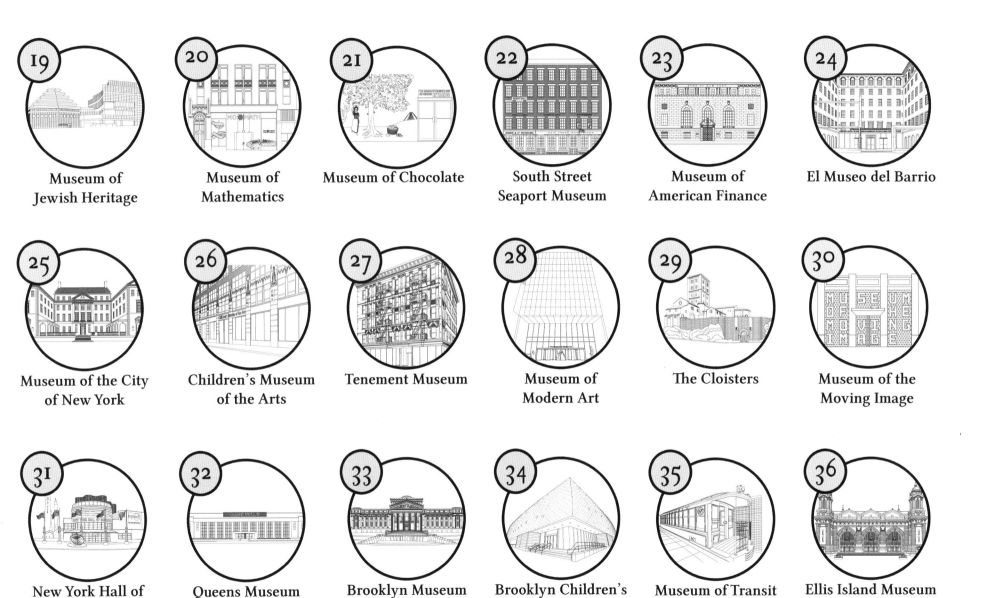

19 Museum of Jewish Heritage

20 Museum of Mathematics

21 Museum of Chocolate

22 South Street Seaport Museum

23 Museum of American Finance

24 El Museo del Barrio

25 Museum of the City of New York

26 Children's Museum of the Arts

27 Tenement Museum

28 Museum of Modern Art

29 The Cloisters

30 Museum of the Moving Image

31 New York Hall of Science

32 Queens Museum

33 Brooklyn Museum

34 Brooklyn Children's Museum

35 Museum of Transit

36 Ellis Island Museum

NEUE GALERIE

Neue Galerie New York is a museum devoted to early twentieth-century German and Austrian art and design. The collection features art from early twentieth century German and Austrian art movements. Serge Sabarsky and Ronald Lauder conceived Neue Galerie New York to share their passion for Modern German and Austrian art, and wanted to open a museum to showcase them. After Sabarsky died in 1996, Lauder created Neue Galerie New York. The building housing Neue Galerie New York is located at 1048 Fifth Avenue at 86th Street. Completed by Carrère and Hastings in 1914, it has been designated a landmark by the New York Landmarks Commission and is one of Fifth Avenue's most illustrious buildings. Mrs. Cornelius Vanderbilt III and the Yivo Institute occupied it before Ronald Lauder and Serge Sabarsky bought it in 1994. Annabelle Selldorf oversaw the building's renovation, restoring 1048 Fifth Avenue to its original state, while adapting it to stringent museum standards with regard to displaying and preserving works of art.

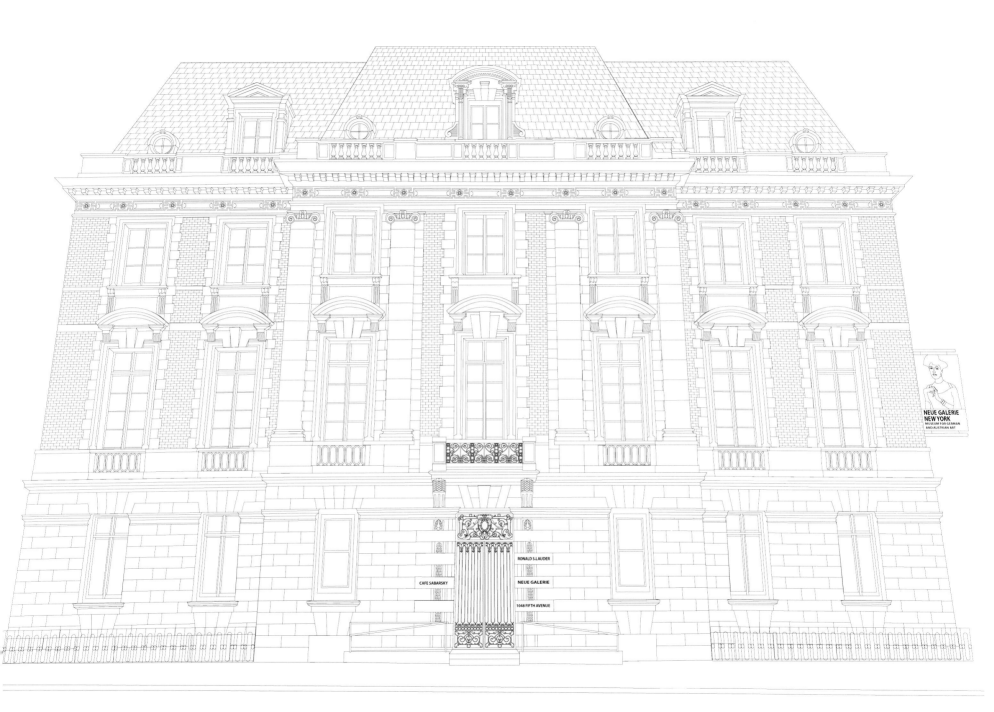

CAFE SABARSKY

RONALD S.LAUDER

NEUE GALERIE

1048 FIFTH AVENUE

NEUE GALERIE
NEW YORK
MUSEUM FOR GERMAN
AND AUSTRIAN ART

UKRAINIAN INSTITUTE OF AMERICA

Located on the corner of 79th Street and Fifth Avenue, the stunning Fletcher-Sinclair mansion contains the Ukrainian Institute of America. The mansion itself dates back to 1898, when Isaac Fletcher hired C.P.H. Gilbert to build a French-style house. Harry Sinclair bought the Fletcher Mansion in 1920 and sold it in 1930 to Peter Stuyvesant's last direct male descendant, Augustus Van Horne Stuyvesant, Jr., who occupied the mansion until his sister died in 1938. In 1948, William Dzus founded the Ukrainian Institute of America, Inc. at West Islip, to promote Ukrainian art and culture. In 1955, the Ukrainian Institute of America moved to New York City, and bought the Fletcher-Sinclair Mansion. In June 1962, the Ukrainian Institute of America became a landmark. The Ukrainian Institute of America has sponsored many events, such as theatrical performances, conferences, art festivals, seminars showcasing news and political events in Ukraine, exhibits featuring the Chernobyl nuclear disaster and the Holodomor Genocide, and a classical music concert series.

THE
UKRAINIAN INSTITUTE
OF AMERICA

Smithsonian Design Museum

COOPER HEWITT

Founded in 1897 by Peter Cooper's granddaughters Sarah and Eleanor Hewitt, Cooper Hewitt, Smithsonian Design Museum is housed in Andrew Carnegie's former home. Built from 1899 to 1902, the mansion was the United States' first private home to have a structural steel frame and one of New York State's first edifices to have a residential Otis passenger elevator. The building became a landmark in 1974, and it opened in 1976 as the Smithsonian Institution's Cooper-Hewitt Museum. From 2011 to 2014, Cooper Hewitt closed for renovations, increasing its exhibition space, reimagining its exhibits, and implementing new technologies. In 2014, the museum was renamed Cooper Hewitt, Smithsonian Design Museum. Cooper Hewitt, Smithsonian Design Museum advances the public understanding of design through offering interactive exhibits, four floors of galleries, a collection of 210,000 design objects, and online resources. As a result, Cooper-Hewitt is a museum that stands as a paradigm for design thinking and problem solving.

FRICK COLLECTION

Housed in Henry Frick's New York City mansion, the Frick Collection serves as a monument to one of America's great art collectors. The Collection's distinct art galleries are arranged without regard to period or national origin. In 1906, Frick acquired a site on Fifth Avenue between 70th and 71st Streets, which became his New York mansion in 1914. The mansion housed Frick's artworks, and was planned to become a museum following the deaths of him and his wife. Before Frick died in 1919, he left the house, artworks, and furnishings as The Frick Collection. After her father died in 1919, Helen Frick served as the Collection's founding trustee and created the Frick Art Reference Library in 1920. It became home to William Dinsmoor's Committee on the Protection of Cultural Treasures in War Areas, who mapped and indexed monuments, buildings and artworks for the Allies to spare during bombing runs in World War II. The Frick Collection opened in 1935, fulfilling Henry Frick's intention to present his art collection and mansion to New York City.

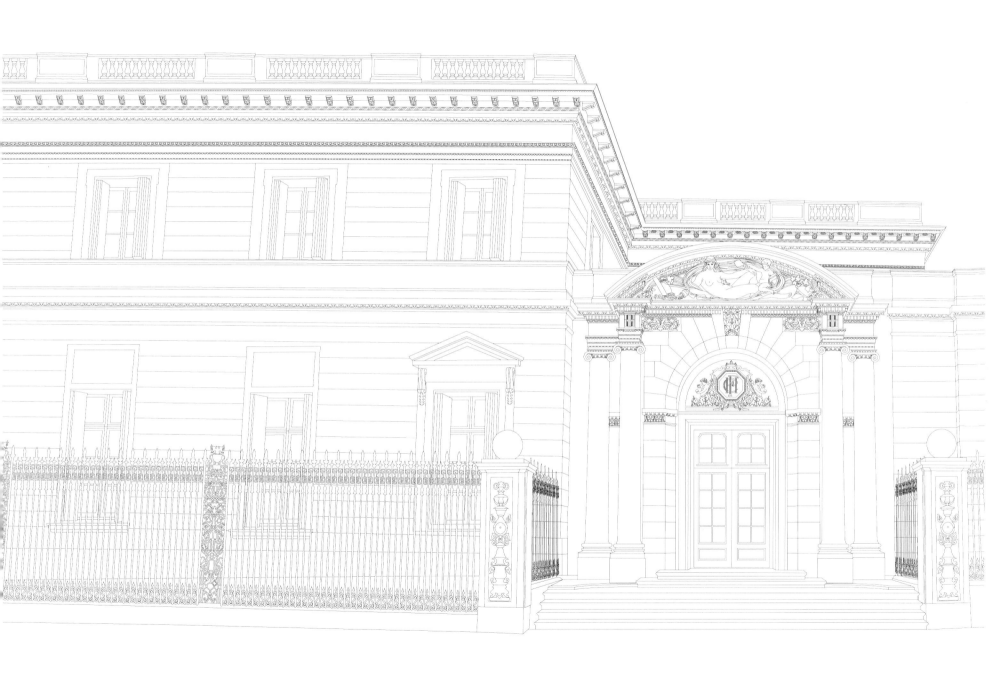

GUGGENHEIM MUSEUM

In 1943, Solomon Guggenheim hired Frank Lloyd Wright to design a home for the Museum of Non-Objective Painting's art collection. The museum broke ground in August 1956 and opened on October 21st, 1959. William Wesley Peters, Wright's son-in-law, completed a four-story tower in 1968. In 1978, Richard Meier created the Aye Simon Reading Room. In 1990, the Landmark Preservation Commission selected the Guggenheim Museum as a New York City Landmark. The Frank Lloyd Wright building's exterior restoration began in 2005 and ended in 2008, when the United States Secretary of the Interior and the National Park Service designated the Guggenheim Museum as a National Historic Landmark. The Guggenheim celebrated its 50th anniversary and opened the Wright restaurant in 2009. In 2015, the Solomon R. Guggenheim Museum was nominated to the U.N's Educational, Scientific and Cultural Organization World Heritage List.

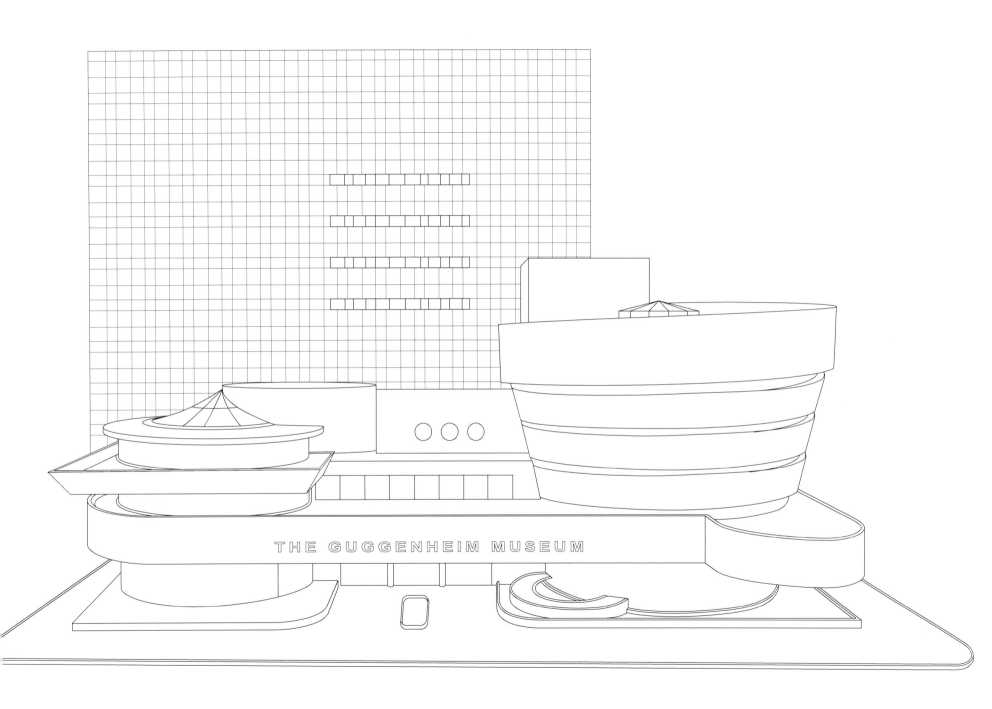

THE GUGGENHEIM MUSEUM

METROPOLITAN MUSEUM OF ART

On April 13th, 1870, the Metropolitan Museum of Art opened in the Dodworth Building at 681 Fifth Avenue. On March 30th, 1880, the Met opened on Fifth Avenue and 82nd Street, and added its Beaux-Arts facade in December 1902. In 1910, the Met was the world's first public institution to obtain Henri Matisse's artwork. The Egyptian hippo statue/ unofficial mascot "William" was acquired in 1917. The Museum now displays 26,000 Egyptian objects, making it the largest Egyptian art collection outside of Cairo. In 1971, Kevin Roche and John Dinkeloo designed wings to hold modern, Oceanic, African, Renaissance, Impressionist, American, and European art. The Met opened the Korean art gallery in 1998, the Oceanic, Native North American, Nineteenth and early Twentieth-Century art galleries in 2007, and the Central and South Asian art galleries in 2011. In 2016, 6.7 million people visited the Met Fifth Avenue and its two branches, the Met Breuer and the Cloisters. The Met always serves the broadest possible audience.

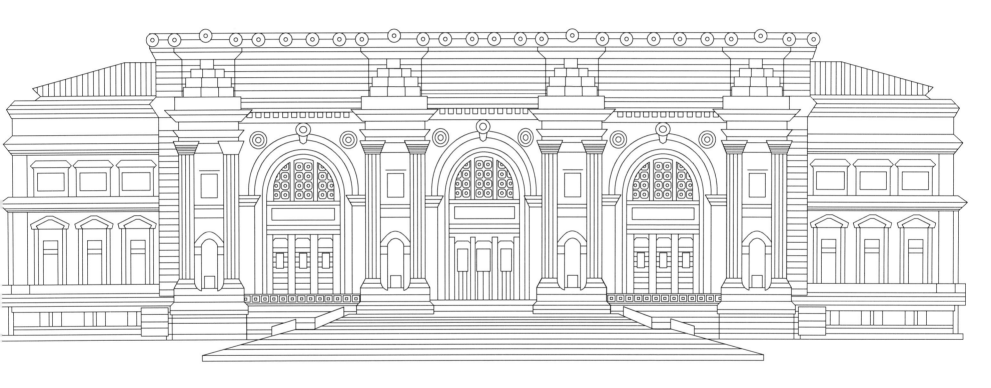

JEWISH MUSEUM

Founded in 1904, the Jewish Museum is one of the world's oldest Jewish museums and was the first museum of its kind in the United States. The Museum moved to the former home of noted philanthropist Felix Warburg at 1109 Fifth Avenue on 92nd Street in 1947. Devoted to exploring art and Jewish culture for people of all backgrounds, the Jewish Museum has organized seminal exhibits like The Dreyfus Affair: Art, Truth and Justice; Bridges and Boundaries: African Americans and American Jews; Culture and Continuity: The Jewish Journey, Florine Stettheimer: Painting Poetry; and Modigliani Unmasked. The Museum maintains a collection of nearly 30,000 artworks, ceremonial objects, and media reflecting the entire global Jewish experience, while also offering educational exhibits and programs for everyone. With its unparalleled collection and dynamic exhibitions, the Museum presents art and Jewish cultural objects, affirming universal values that are shared among people of all faiths and backgrounds.

AMERICAN MUSEUM
ᵒ NATURAL HISTORY

AMERICAN MUSEUM OF NATURAL HISTORY

Created in 1869, the American Museum of Natural History is one of the world's preeminent scientific and cultural institutions. Located between West 77th and 81st Streets next to Central Park, the Museum advances its mission to discover, interpret, and disseminate information about human cultures, the natural world, and the universe through a wide-ranging program of scientific research, education, and exhibition. The Museum's renowned exhibits and scientific collections serve as a field guide to the entire planet and present a panorama of the world's cultures. The landmark Museum includes such fascinating areas as the Rose Center for Earth and Space, which contains the massive Hayden Sphere and Space Theater, and the Theodore Roosevelt Rotunda, which exhibits the world's highest freestanding dinosaur display. As the basis for the Night at the Museum film trilogy, the Museum is *the* New York institution.

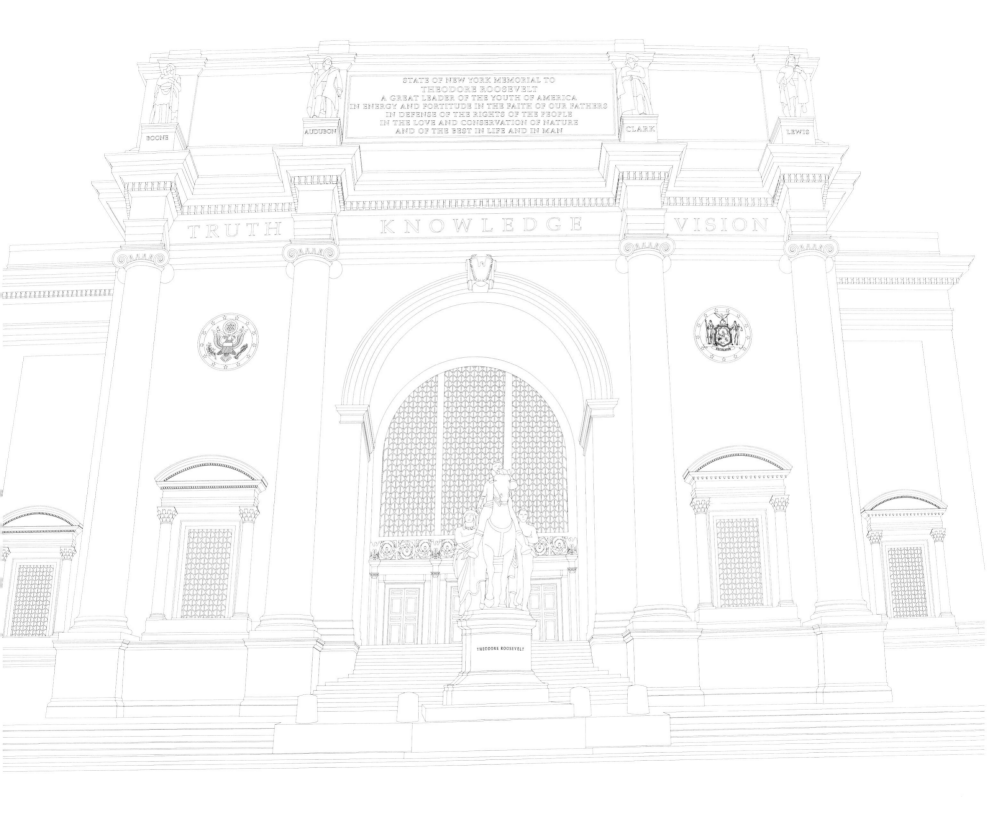

NEW-YORK HISTORICAL SOCIETY

One of America's leading cultural institutions, the New York Historical Society presents exhibits and programs that reveal history's influence on today's world. Founded in 1804 to explore the city's sociopolitical and cultural history, New York Historical is recognized for exhibits like Alexander Hamilton: The Man Who Made Modern America, Slavery in New York, Grant and Lee in War and Peace, and WWII and NYC. It includes the Patricia Klingenstein Library, the Henry Luce III Center, the DiMenna Children's History Museum, and the Gilder Lehrman Collection. New York Historical's renovations include new galleries and exhibit spaces, the Henry Luce III Center, a reading room, and a facility to house the Gilder Lehrman Collection's letters and manuscripts. Completed in November 2011, New York Historical's renovation enhanced its status as one of the nation's premier cultural and educational resources.

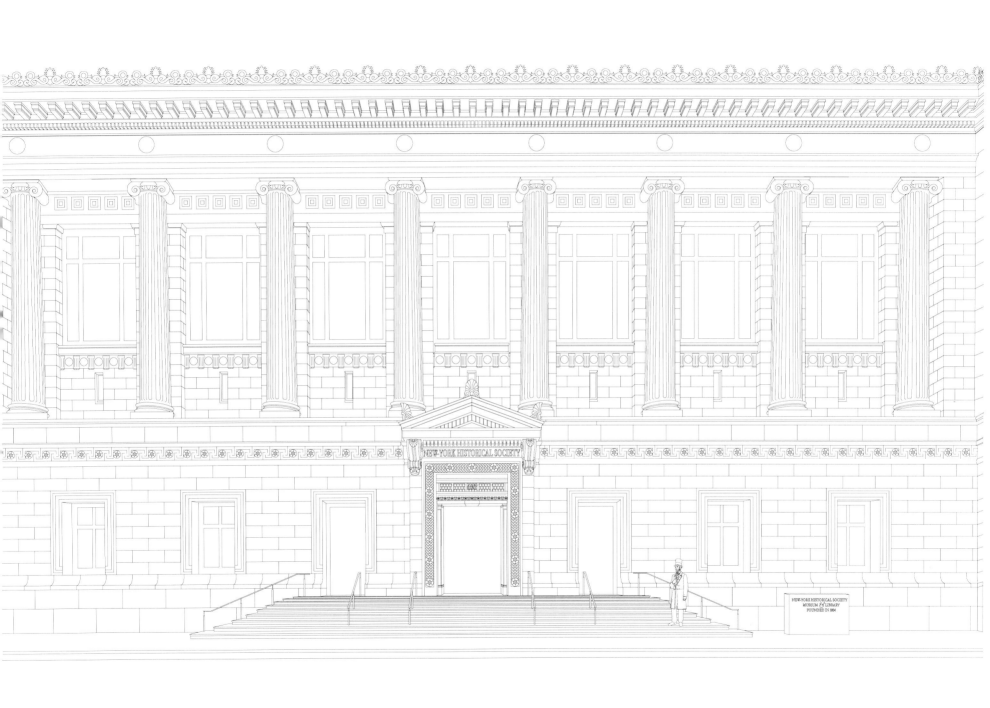

museum of arts and design

MAD MUSEUM

The Museum of Arts and Design explores the value of making across all fields of contemporary creative practice. The Museum focuses on the ways in which artists and designers transform the world around us, through processes ranging from the artisanal to the digital. MAD's exhibition program is dedicated to creativity and craftsmanship, and demonstrates the limitless potential of materials and techniques when used by gifted and innovative artists. The Museum's permanent collection is global in scope and includes art, craft, and design from 1950 to the present day. At the center of the Museum's mission is education. The Museum houses classrooms and studios for master classes, seminars, and workshops for students, families, and adults. Three open studios engage visitors in the creative processes of artists at work and enhance the exhibition programs. Lectures, films, performances, and symposia related to the Museum's collection and subjects across the full spectrum of making practices are held in a renovated 144-seat auditorium.

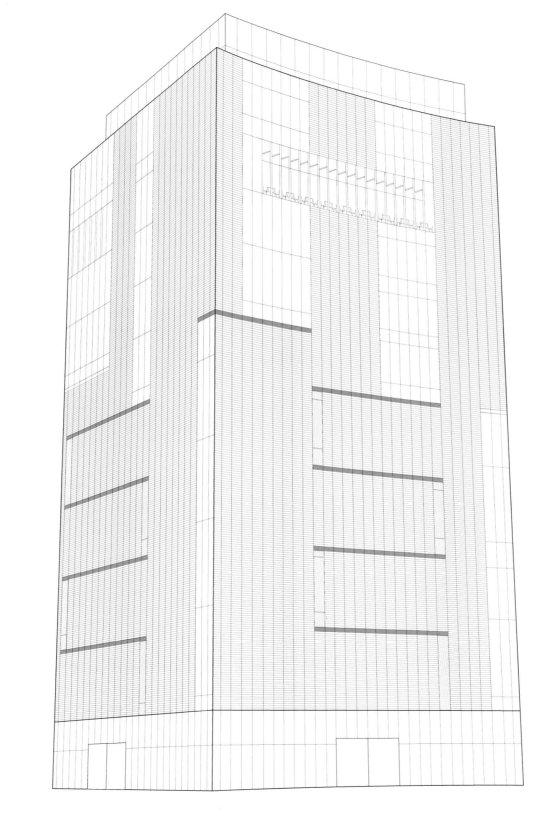

Children's Museum of Manhattan

CHILDREN'S MUSEUM OF MANHATTAN

By creating experiences through exhibits, classes, workshops, performances, and festivals at the intersection of art, sciences, and the humanities, the Children's Museum of Manhattan helps children and families thrive. Their programs and exhibits address the ways children learn and helps parents understand and support their child's development. The Museum's areas of focus are education, creativity, health, and world cultures. Founded in 1973 to bring the arts to New York City public schools, the Children's Museum serves a diverse audience. As a citywide resource and a destination for visitors from around the world, each year over 350,000 people visit their learning facility. Visitors enjoy over 80 free workshops, classes, and performances.

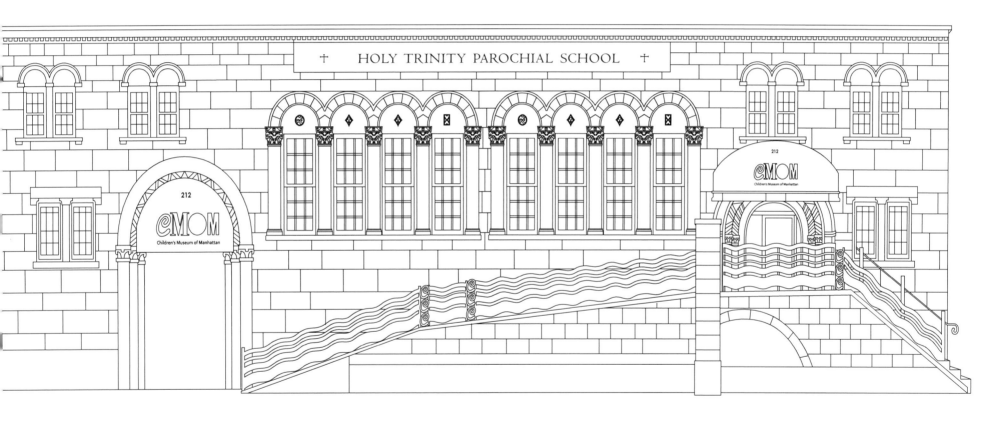

AMERICAN FOLK ART MUSEUM

The American Folk Art Museum is the premier institution devoted to the creative expressions of self-taught artists. Since 1961, the American Folk Art Museum has been shaping the understanding of art by the self-taught through its exhibits, publications, and programs. As a scholastic center and by showcasing the creativity of experienced individuals, the museum considers the socio-historical, and artistic context of American culture. Its collection includes over eight thousand artworks dating from the eighteenth century to the present, from portraits and quilts to works by living self-taught artists in other mediums. The museum hosts a wide array of events for every level of interest. Programs including lectures, discussions, and symposia make experts and cultural leaders accessible to the public. Workshops and musical performances are offered in the galleries weekly, and school, camp, teen, and adult programs take place throughout the year. The museum is dedicated to making the study of folk and self-taught art available to and meaningful for all.

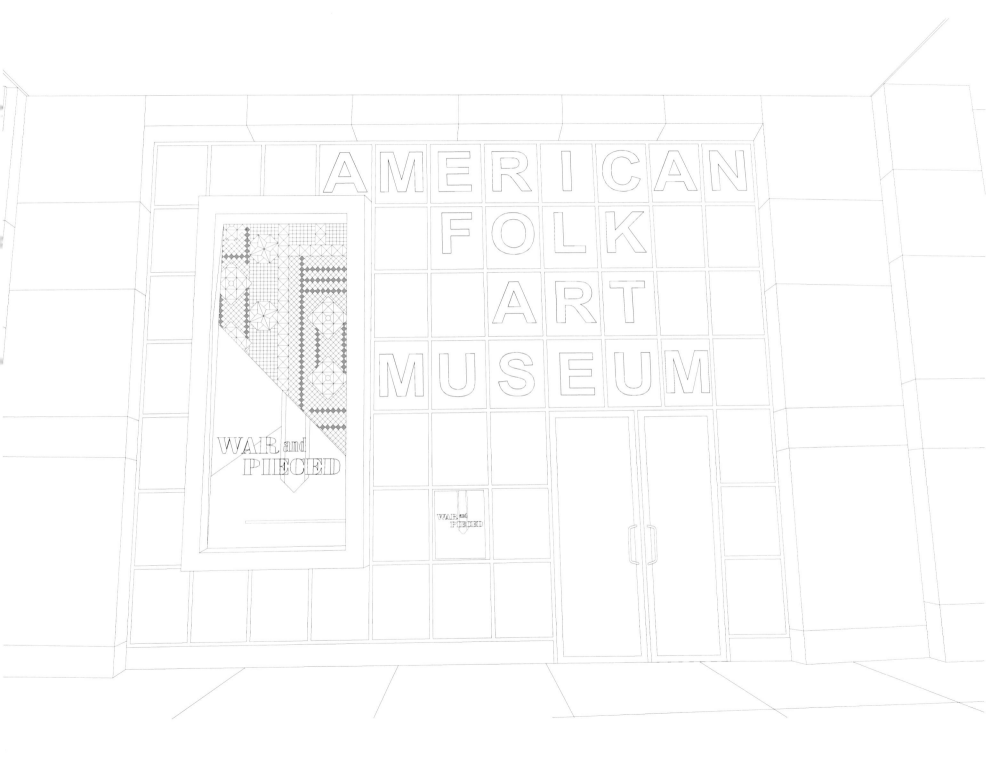

MUSEUM AT ELDRIDGE STREET

The Museum at Eldridge Street's Synagogue is a vital part of the Lower East Side's Jewish history. Opening in 1887, the Synagogue was descended from America's first Russian Jewish congregation. It is now the only marker left of the old Lower East Side. The synagogue was built during a time when over 2 million Jews came to the United States. 85 percent of Eastern European Jewish immigrants came to New York City, and 75 percent of them settled on the Lower East Side. The Eldridge Street Synagogue was a spiritual home for Russian, Polish, and Lithuanian immigrants for fifty years. However, it declined after the 1924 Immigrant Quota Laws and the exodus to the outer boroughs. In 1986, the Eldridge Street Project formed to save the synagogue, repairing the building, and securing it a National Historic Landmark designation in 1996. The Museum completed the Synagogue's restoration in 2007 and built a visitor center in 2014. Today the Museum at Eldridge Street welcomes people for tours, programs, concerts, lectures, festivals and other events.

THE NEW MUSEUM

Founded by Marcia Tucker in 1977, the New Museum is a catalyst for dialogue between artists and the public by presenting works of living artists who do not have public exposure or critical acceptance. In 1980, the New Museum launched the High School Art Program to engage teenagers in contemporary art. 1982's "Extended Sensibilities: Homosexual Presence in Contemporary Art" was the first gay and lesbian art exhibit. In 1983, the New Museum moved into the Astor Building at 583 Broadway. In 1985, Larry Aldrich donated the SoHo Center for the Visual Arts Library to the New Museum. Made in response to the AIDS crisis, 1987's "Let the Record Show" had a SILENCE= DEATH sign. 1990's "The Decade Show: Frameworks of Identity in the 1980s" was presented with the Museum of Contemporary Hispanic Art and Harlem's Studio Museum. In 2003, the New Museum selected Kazuyo Sejima + Ryue Nishizawa /SANAA Ltd. to design 235 Bowery, which opened in 2007.

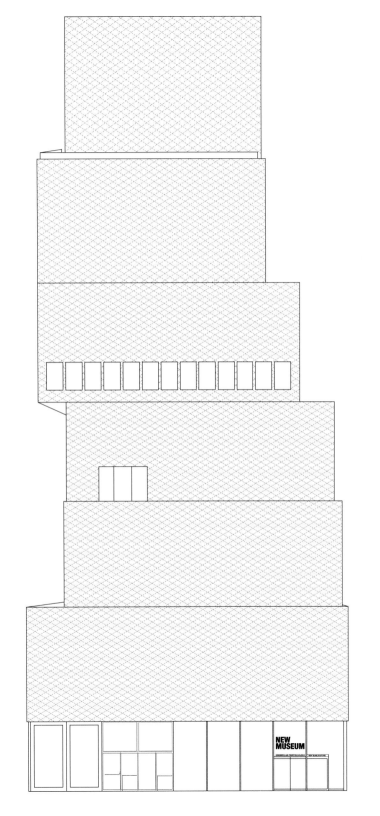

SEA, AIR & SPACE MUSEUM COMPLEX

INTREPID SEA, AIR & SPACE MUSEUM

The USS Intrepid began construction on December 1st, 1941. Intrepid served the U.S. Navy for over three decades, playing a role in World War II, the Cold War, the Space Race, and the Vietnam War. After it retired, Intrepid was mothballed in 1974 and it later opened as a museum, where its history inspires visitors everywhere. The USS Intrepid was authorized on August 16th, 1943. In World War II, Intrepid attacked Truk Lagoon, and contributed in the Battles of Leyte Gulf and Okinawa. The U.S. Navy put Intrepid on reserves at the end of 1945, Intrepid reopened on June 18th, 1954. Intrepid then served as a recovery vessel for the Mercury-Atlas 7 and Gemini 3 space programs. From 1966 to 1969, Intrepid served in Vietnam, mainly for Operation Rolling Thunder. On March 15th, 1974, the Intrepid was retired. Zachary Fisher transformed Intrepid into the Intrepid Sea, Air and Space Museum in 1982, and it became a National Historic Landmark in 1986. The Intrepid Museum promotes its history to honor its heroes, educate the public, and inspire the youth.

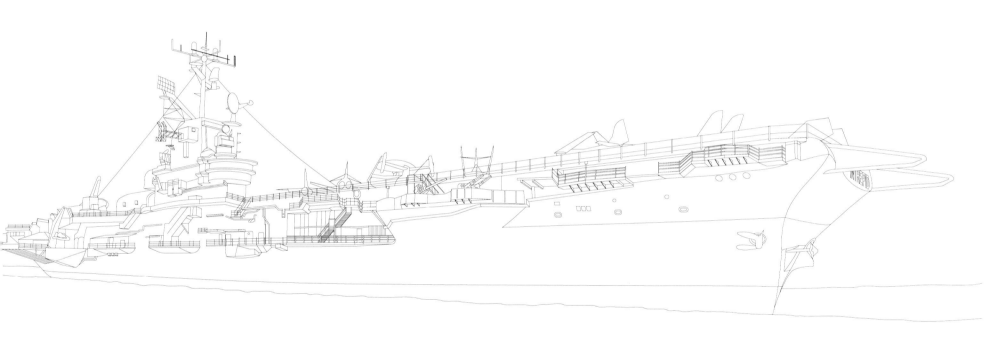

NEW YORK CITY FIRE MUSEUM

The New York City Fire Museum collects, preserves, and presents New York's fire service's historical heritage. The FDNY's original museum opened as the Fire College Museum in Long Island City in 1934. In 1959, the collection moved to 100 Duane Street, which was moved out in 1981 due to an additional collection of fire ephemerae. In 1987, the New York City Fire Museum opened at Engine Company No. 30 on Spring Street. Displays illustrate firefighting's evolution, from Peter Stuyvesant's New Amsterdam bucket brigades to more modern equipment. The Museum also houses a memorial to the 343 FDNY members who sacrificed their lives on 9/11 and houses artifacts from the World Trade Center site. Retired FDNY firefighters relate their stories with the help of the Museum's collection. In 2015, the New York City Fire Museum received a Charter from the NYS Department of Education, giving the museum the recognition it deserves as a cultural and historical institution.

MUSEUM OF THE AMERICAN INDIAN

A multifaceted cultural enterprise, the National Museum of the American Indian is an active component of the Smithsonian Institution, the world's largest museum complex. The NMAI cares for one of the world's most expansive Native artifact collections. The National Museum of the American Indian operates three facilities. The museum on the National Mall in Washington, D.C., offers exhibit galleries and spaces for performances, lectures, research, and education. The George Gustav Heye Center in New York City houses exhibits, research, activities, and performing arts programs. The Cultural Resources Center in Suitland, Maryland, houses collections, digital imaging programs, and research facilities. The NMAI's off-site outreach efforts include websites, traveling exhibitions, and community programs. Since 1989, the NMAI has been committed to bringing Native voices to the public. The NMAI acts as a resource for the hemisphere's Native communities and serves the public as a conduit to Native cultures in all their richness, depth, and diversity.

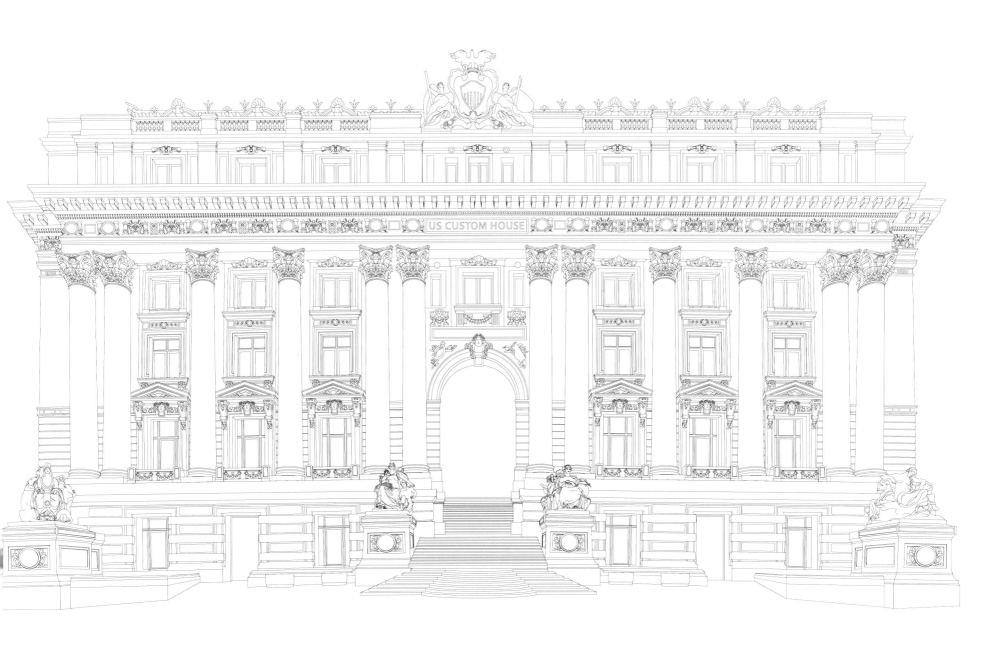

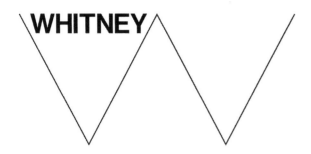

THE WHITNEY MUSEUM OF AMERICAN ART

As the preeminent institution devoted to American art, the Whitney Museum of American Art presents twentieth-century and contemporary art focusing on works by living artists. The Whitney was the first museum dedicated to living American artists and the first New York museum to present a major video art exhibit. Leading American art patron Gertrude Whitney created the Whitney Museum of American Art to advocate for living American artists. In 1914, Whitney established the Whitney Studio in Greenwich Village, and collected over 500 works by 1929. The Whitney Museum of American Art was founded in 1930, opened in 1931 in Greenwich Village, and then moved to West 54th Street in 1954 and the Breuer building on Madison Avenue at 75th Street in 1966, which ended its programming on October 20th, 2014. The Whitney's Gansevoort Street building opened on May 1st, 2015, providing an expansive view of its modern American art collection.

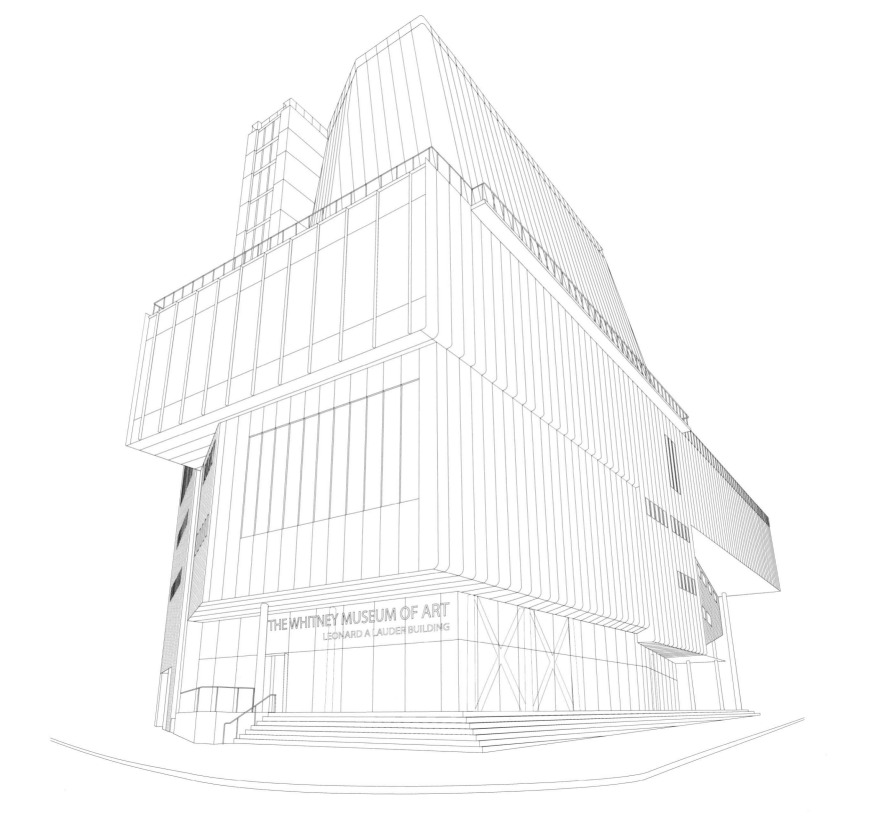

MUSEUM OF JEWISH HERITAGE

Anchoring Manhattan's southern tip, the Museum of Jewish Heritage is a public American institution with strong Jewish roots. Its six-sided shape and six-tiered roof are reminders of the six million Jews who died in the Holocaust and of the six-pointed Star of David that symbolizes the Museum's promise to represent Jewish life and culture. In 1986, the Museum of Jewish Heritage's dedication was held in Battery Park City. In 1994, the Museum had its groundbreaking. On September 15th, 1997, the Museum of Jewish Heritage opened. The Robert Morgenthau Wing opened in 2003. In 2004 and 2005, the American Association of Museums honored the Museum's exhibits *Ours to Fight For: American Jews in the Second World War* and *Daring to Resist: Jewish Defiance in the Holocaust.* In 2009, the Pickman Keeping History Center and Voices of Liberty opened. In 2016, the Museum established the Center for the Study of Anti-Semitism. In 2017, the Museum presented a livestream reading of Elie Wiese's "Night" for International Holocaust Remembrance Day.

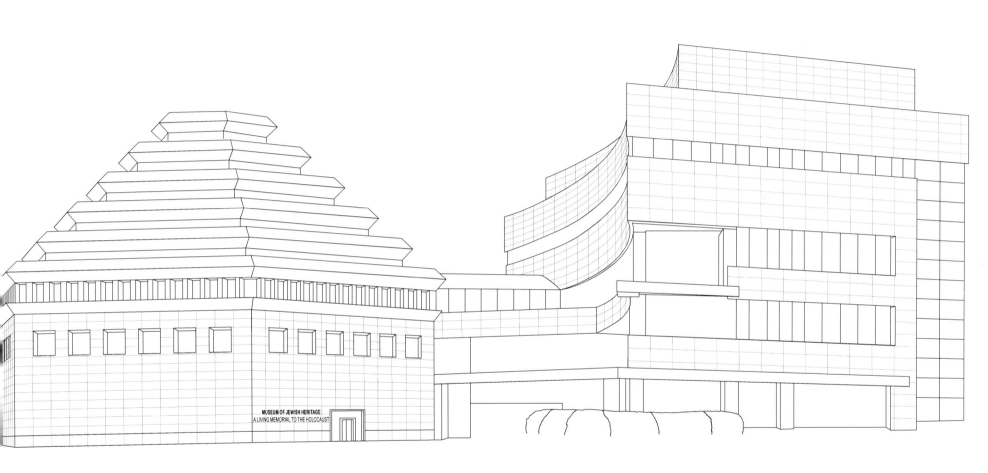

MUSEUM OF JEWISH HERITAGE
A LIVING MEMORIAL TO THE HOLOCAUST

NATIONAL MUSEUM OF MATHEMATICS

MUSEUM OF MATHEMATICS

The National Museum of Mathematics strives to enhance the public understanding and perception of mathematics through its dynamic exhibits and programs, which helps to present the evolving, creative, human, and aesthetic nature of mathematics. The National Museum of Mathematics began in response to the Goudreau Museum of mathematics' closing in Long Island. A group of interested parties met in 2008 to create a museum of mathematics that would go beyond the Goudreau in scope and methodology. The group discovered that there was no museum of mathematics in the United States, and yet there was much demand for hands-on math programming. The National Museum of Mathematics is Manhattan's only hands-on science center and the only mathematics Museum in North America, creating such works as the popular traveling Math Midway exhibit and the largest public outdoor demonstration of the Pythagorean Theorem ever.

MUSEUM OF CHOCOLATE

The Museum of Chocolate is New York's first-ever chocolate museum! Visitors will discover in the 5,000 sq. foot museum the story of chocolate and its journey from tree to bar through a tour of original artifacts, eight premium tastings, including original Mayan hot chocolate freshly ground by hand, and a bon-bon making demonstration, offering a deliciously educational experience for families, children, and chocolate lovers. The museum also features a kid's corner, an educational space where children can dig for "undiscovered artifacts" in a sand pit and play chocolate shop proprietor with a toy kitchen and cash register. Children aged 4 to 12 can also participate in a sticker game where if they guess correctly, they will be given a chocolate treat. For an additional cost to the museum admission, taught by a professional chocolatier, customers may schedule in advance a beginner chocolate making experience where they will be able to sample their own handiwork and take their creations home.

SOUTH STREET SEAPORT MUSEUM

South Street Seaport Museum is a cultural institution dedicated to telling New York's story in developing the United States. The Museum uses its historic buildings and ships to provide interactive exhibits, education, and experiences. The Museum's collections consist of over 26,500 objects documenting New York's rise as a port city and its role in developing the United States' economy through its social and architectural landscapes. The collections include maritime oil paintings, printing presses, over 6,000 drawings photographs, and prints of New York City, manuscripts, 2,400 ship models, carved whale bones, navigational instruments, and historical objects related to the Seaport's trade. South Street Seaport Museum also includes the Titanic Memorial Lighthouse, two anchors, and the New York Central No. 31 railroad barge pilothouse. In 2017, the Museum celebrated its 50th anniversary.

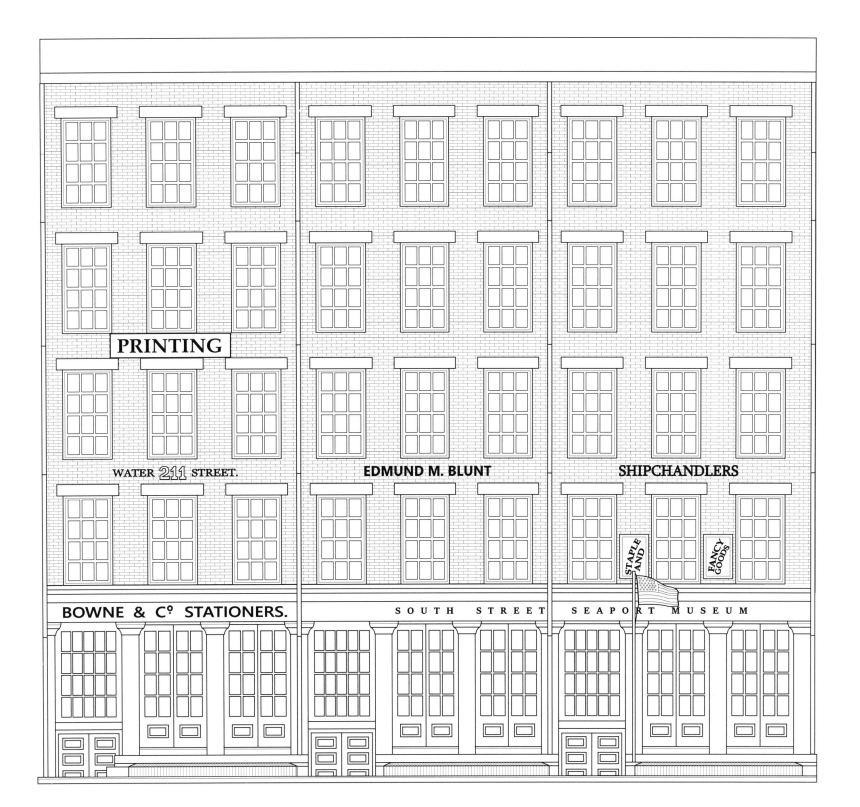

PRINTING

WATER 211 STREET.

EDMUND M. BLUNT

SHIPCHANDLERS

STAPLE AND

FANCY GOODS

BOWNE & Cº STATIONERS.

SOUTH STREET SEAPORT MUSEUM

MUSEUM OF AMERICAN FINANCE

The Museum of American Finance, an affiliate of the Smithsonian Institution, is the nation's only independent museum dedicated to celebrating the spirit of entrepreneurship and the democratic free market tradition which have made New York City the financial capital of the world. Founded in response to the Crash of 1987, the Museum's core mission is to preserve, exhibit and teach about American finance and financial history. Housed in an historic bank building on Wall Street, the Museum's magnificent grand mezzanine banking hall provides an ideal setting for permanent exhibits on the financial markets, money, banking, entrepreneurship and Alexander Hamilton. Recent temporary exhibits have included "Worth Its Weight: Gold from the Ground Up," "Women of Wall Street" and "For the Love of Money: Blacks on US Currency."

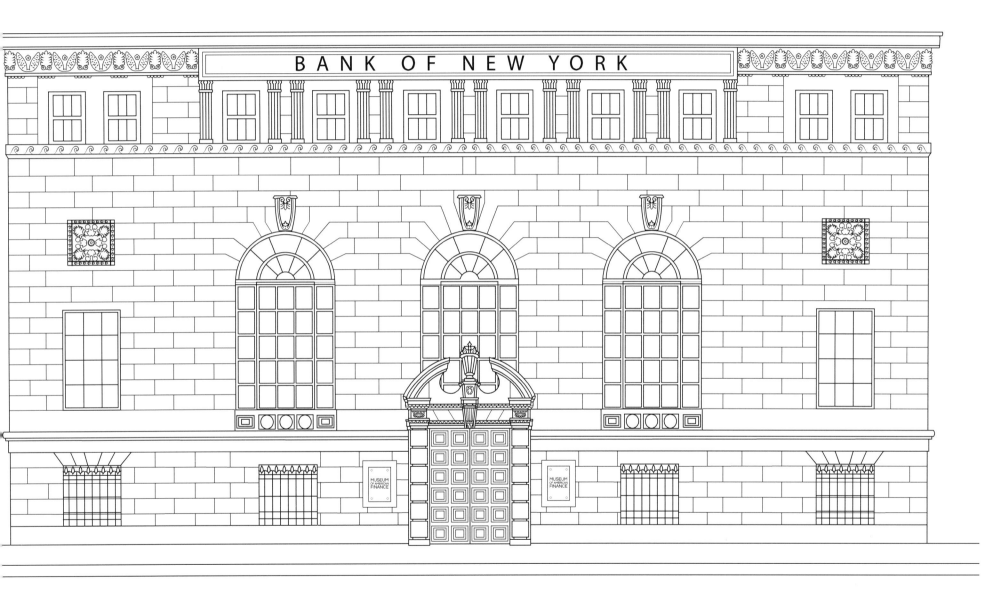

DEL BARRIO
NEW YORK

EL MUSEO DEL BARRIO

Founded in 1969 by Raphael Ortiz, El Museo del Barrio is New York's leading Latino cultural institution, welcoming visitors to discover the artistic landscape of Latino, Caribbean, and Latin American cultures through its mammoth collections and exhibits. El Museo's mission is to present and preserve the art and culture of Puerto Ricans and all Latin Americans in the United States. With a purpose to collect, preserve, exhibit, and interpret Caribbean and Latin American art and artifacts, enhance the identity and knowledge of Caribbeans and Latin Americans by educating them in their heritage and bringing art and artists into their communities, and provide a forum that promotes an appreciation of Caribbean and Latin American art and culture, El Museo educates the public in Caribbean and Latin American arts and cultural history, creating generations of museumgoers and satisfying their interest in Caribbean and Latin American art.

A MUSEUM IS A SCHOOL: THE ARTIST LEARNS TO COMMUNICATE. THE PUBLIC LEARNS TO MAKE CONNECTIONS

HECKSCHER BUILDING

MUSEUM OF THE CITY OF NEW YORK

The Museum of the City of New York celebrates the city, educating the public about its character, heritage, and transformation. Founded in 1923 by Henry Collins Brown, the Museum connects New York City's past, present, and future through exhibits, programs, publications, and collections. The Museum was initially housed in Gracie Mansion, the future residence of New York City's Mayor. For the Museum new home, the City offered land on Fifth Avenue on 103rd and 104th Streets and construction for the building started in 1929 and was completed in 1932. During the next few decades, the Museum amassed items like Eugene O'Neill's manuscripts, a room of Duncan Phyfe furniture, Jacob Riis' glass negatives, a suit worn to George Washington's Inaugural Ball, and the Carrie Walter Stettheimer dollhouse, which contains a miniature work by Marcel Duchamp. Today the Museum's collection contains around 750,000 objects, including prints, costumes, photographs, decorative arts, paintings, sculpture, toys, and memorabilia.

Children's Museum of the Arts

CHILDREN'S MUSEUM OF THE ARTS

The Children's Museum of the Arts introduces children and their families to the power of the arts by providing opportunities to make art side-by-side with artists. Founded in 1988 by Kathleen Schneider, the museum has been located in SoHo since its inception. As CMA's audience grew, its young artists grew as well, eventually outgrowing the facility on Lafayette Street. CMA needed a larger space to expand its' programming, reaching more communities and kids up to age 15. In 2010, CMA broke ground on a former loading dock west of SoHo, working with architects and developers to create a state-of-the art facility that would benefit a range of ages and abilities. Children's Museum of the Arts opened its new 10,000sq ft. home on Charlton Street in 2011. Since then, CMA has served hundreds of thousands of children and families, free of charge.

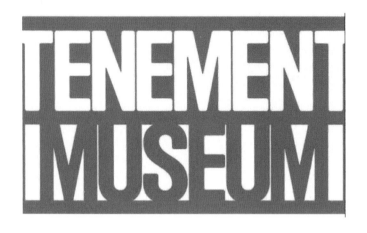

TENEMENT MUSEUM

Built on Manhattan's Lower East Side in 1863, 97 Orchard Street was home to nearly 7000 immigrants. In recognizing its importance, the Tenement Museum preserves and interprets the history of immigration via the experiences of those who settled in Manhattan's Lower East Side, forges connections between visitors and immigrants, and enhances gratitude for how immigration shapes America's national identity. In 1988, Ruth Abram and Anita Jacobson stumbled upon a perfect time capsule in 97 Orchard Street. Researchers scavenged through 97 Orchard and combed through archives about tenants and tenement life. The Museum then began restoring the vacant apartments, opened its first in 1992. Over the past 25 years, the Tenement Museum has blossomed from an idea into an institution. They have restored six apartments. In 2007, the Museum bought 103 Orchard Street to serve as a building for the Visitors Center, exhibits, and classrooms.

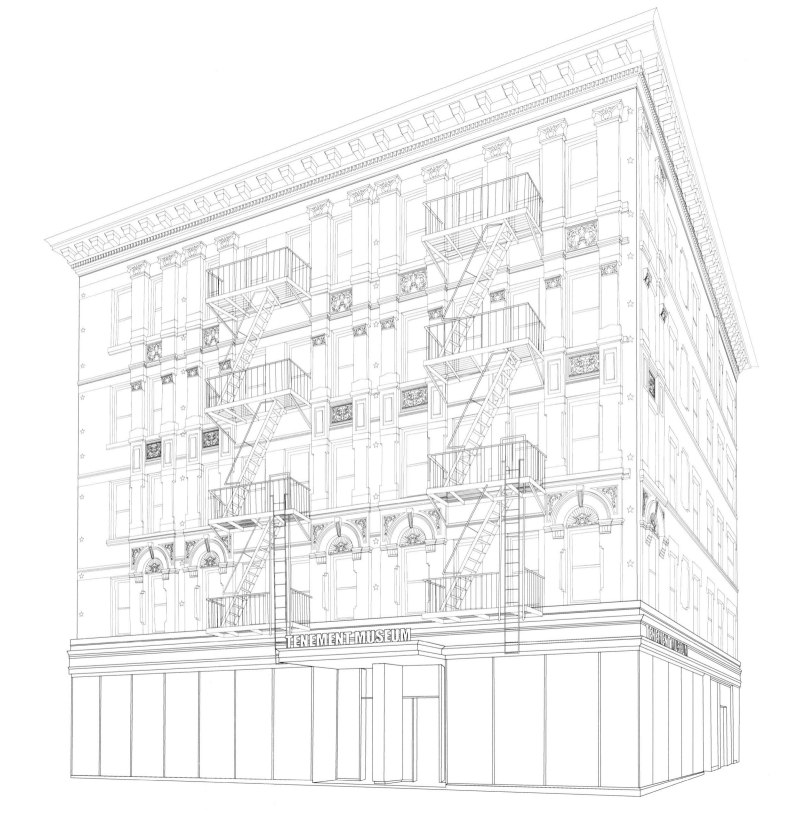

The Museum of Modern Art

MUSEUM OF MODERN ART

In 1929 Miss Lillie Bliss, Mrs. Cornelius Sullivan, and Mrs. John Rockefeller, Jr. created the Museum of Modern Art. Over the next 10 years, the Museum moved three times, and in 1939, it opened in midtown Manhattan. Philip Johnson expanded the museum in the 1950s and 1960s. In 1984, Cesar Pelli's renovation doubled the Museum's gallery space. The Museum of Modern Art's collection has grown to around 200,000 paintings, sculptures, drawings, photographs, artworks, models, and around two million film stills. The Museum's Library contains the world's largest modern art research collection, holding over 320,000 items on over 90,000 artists. The Museum also has a publishing program that has published over 2,500 editions in 35 languages. In 2006, Yoshio Taniguchi nearly doubled MoMA's space for its exhibits and programs. Today, The Museum of Modern Art welcomes millions of visitors yearly. MoMA's exhibits, programs, video library, publications, archival holdings, websites, activities, and events serve the public.

The Museum of Modern Art

THE CLOISTERS

Even though it is a branch of the Metropolitan Museum of Art, The Cloisters at Fort Tryon Park sneaks under New Yorkers' radar. In 1917, John Rockefeller bought the Billings mansion in Fort Tryon Park. In 1925, Rockefeller acquired George Bernard's medieval art collection and then gave it to the Metropolitan Museum of Art. In 1931, he donated the land to the City. Rockefeller had Charles Collens design a museum for the medieval art and artifact collections. French cloisters, stained glass windows, sculptures, columns, and three gardens were integrated in the design. Opening in 1938, the museum grew from Rockefeller's endowments and gifts. The Cloisters begins with the Romanesque Hall, the Langon Chapel, and the Cuxa Cloister and Garden. The Cloisters continues with the Pontaur Chapter House, John Rockefeller's Unicorn Tapestries, the Boppard Room, and the Merode Room, which showcases the Merode Alterpiece, one of the world's most famous Netherlandish paintings. The Cloisters concludes with the Late Gothic Hall and the Bonnefont Cloister and Garden.

MUSEUM OF THE MOVING IMAGE

MUSEUM OF THE MOVING IMAGE

The Museum of the Moving Image advances the understanding, enjoyment, and appreciation of the art, history, technique, and technology of media by presenting exhibits, programs, and moving-image works, as well as collecting and preserving moving-image related artifacts. The Museum maintains the nation's largest collection of artifacts relating to the art, history, and technology of the moving image with an assortment of over 130,000 media artifacts. Since opening out of Paramount's former Astoria Studio complex in 1988, it has been the United States' only museum dedicated to exploring the art, history, and technology of the moving image. The Museum's core exhibit Behind the Screen immerses visitors in the process of making moving images by featuring over 1,400 artifacts, and an array of interactive experiences, material, and artworks. The Museum's recent expansion and renovation project has made it an international center for the appreciation and study of the moving image, and a destination for museumgoers and tourists.

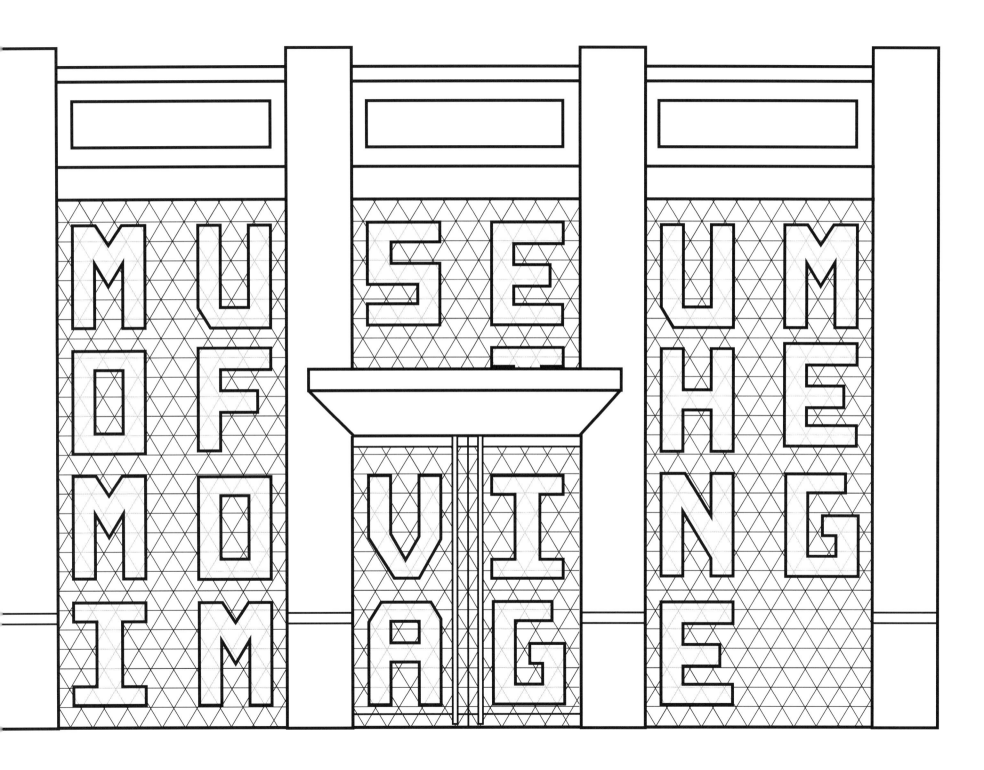

NEW YORK HALL OF SCIENCE

Founded at the 1964–65 World's Fair, the New York Hall of Science has evolved into New York's center for interactive science, serving half a million people a year. The Hall offers hands-on learning through "design-make-play" products and services that make learning about Science, Technology, Engineering, and Math fun. NYSCI's Great Hall rises 100 feet tall with no corners or straight segments and its façade is made up of over 5,000 2-by-3-foot glass panels. When built, the Great Hall was the world's largest poured-in-place concrete structure. By employing youth from their diverse community for their science career ladder program, the museum helps to diversify science and technology fields nationwide.

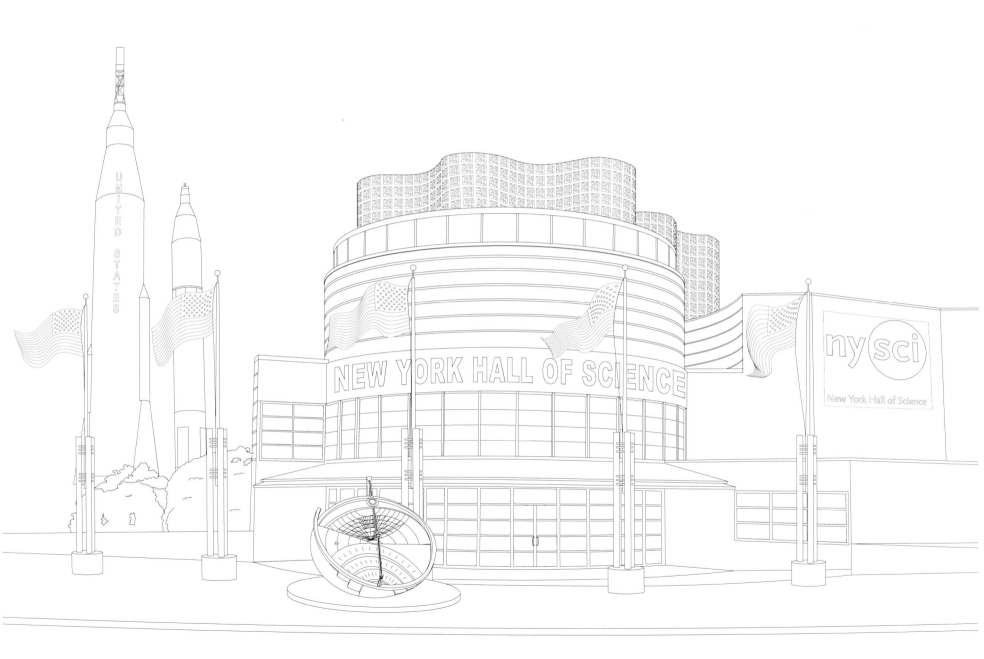

QUEENS MUSEUM

The Queens Museum presents quality visual arts and educational programming for New Yorkers through designing exhibits and programs that promote artistic appreciation and enhance quality of life. Built for the 1939 World's Fair, its home–the New York City Building–housed the United Nations from 1946 to 1950. In the 1964 World's Fair, the Building acquired the New York City Panorama, a model that had every building in the five boroughs. In 1972, the newly formed Queens Museum obtained the New York City Building, which was redesigned by Rafael Viñoly in 1994. In 2013, the Museum doubled its size to 105,000 square feet, and added skylights, a glass staircase, and a LED lit façade. Six gallery spaces allow for concurrent exhibits of different scales and choices. The Queens Museum marries form and function in an open light-filled space that houses ambitious exhibits, progressive educational initiatives, and community-minded programming that engage all constituencies.

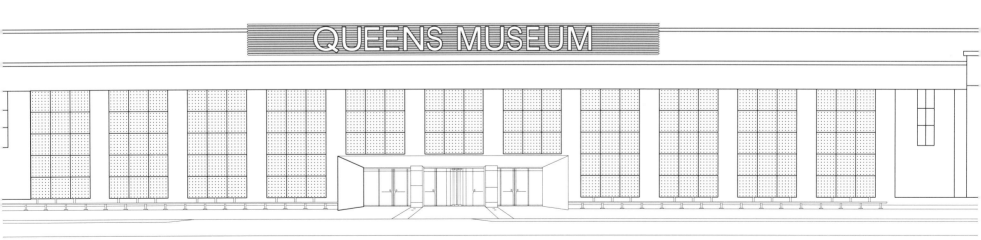

QUEENS MUSEUM

BROOKLYN MUSEUM

Founded in 1823 as the Brooklyn Apprentices' Library, the Brooklyn Museum is one of the United States' oldest and largest art museums. The Museum itself was built from 1895 to 1926, consisting of the west and northeast wings, a central pavilion, a staircase, and the Beaux-Arts Court. In 1977, the Museum was added to the National Register of Historic Places. During the 1990's, the Museum built the Cantor Auditorium and the Schapiro Wing, as well as revamping the Beaux-Arts Court. The Museum's front entrance and plaza contains the glass-encrusted Rubin Pavilion and Lobby, a front stoop, a fountain, and a reflecting pool. In 2007, the Beaux-Arts Court's floor was renovated, adding steel framed glass panels while preserving the mosaic tiled marble floor. The Museum is home to the Elizabeth Sackler Center for Feminist Art, the country's first public space that explores feminist art. Above all else, the Brooklyn Museum is where people can discover dignity and empathy through its exceptional works of art, interesting discussions, and inventive tactics.

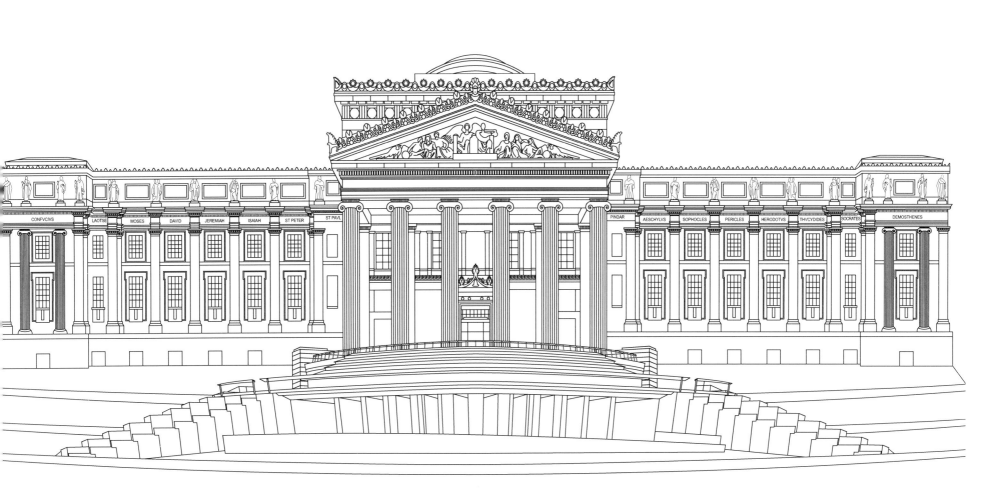

CONFVCIVS   LAOTSE   MOSES   DAVID   JEREMIAH   ISAIAH   ST PETER   ST PAVL   PINDAR   AESCHYLVS   SOPHOCLES   PERICLES   HERODOTVS   THVCYDIDES   SOCRATES   DEMOSTHENES

BROOKLYN CHILDREN'S MUSEUM

Founded in 1899 by the Brooklyn Institute of Arts and Sciences, the Brooklyn Children's Museum is the world's first museum designed expressly for children, emphasizing participatory exhibits that teach children through first-hand experience. The Museum's original home was the Adams Mansion, which was located at Brower Park in Crown Heights. In the Depression, WPA workers prepared dioramas, painted landscapes in exhibits, mounted specimens, and began a Portable Collections Program for the Children's Museum. The Museum's temporary Muse facility redefined museum education by integrating arts, culture and science with social issues. In 1977, the new Brooklyn Children's Museum opened, which then expanded in 2008. The current Museum is New York City's only LEED-certified green museum and one of only a handful of children's museums with a permanent collection, which today includes nearly 30,000 cultural and natural science objects that are utilized in programs, exhibitions, and media.

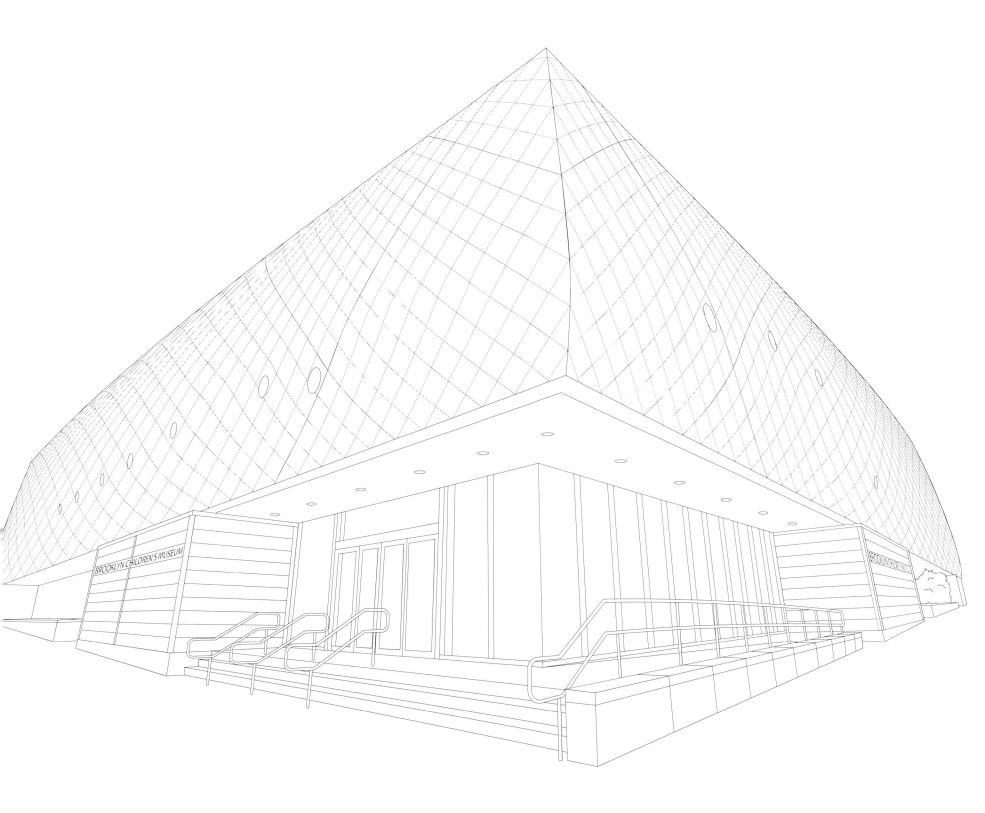

NEW YORK TRANSIT MUSEUM

Founded in 1976, the New York Transit Museum is dedicated to telling and preserving the stories of mass transportation – extraordinary engineering feats, workers who labored in the tunnels over 100 years ago, communities that were drastically transformed, and the ever-evolving technology, design, and ridership of a system that runs 24 hours a day, every day of the year. Housed underground in an authentic 1936 subway station in Downtown Brooklyn, the Transit Museum's working platform level spans a full city block, and is home to a rotating selection of twenty vintage subway and elevated cars dating back to 1907. Visitors can board the vintage cars, sit at the wheel of a city bus, step through a time tunnel of turnstiles, and explore changing exhibits that highlight the cultural, social and technological history – and future – of mass transit.

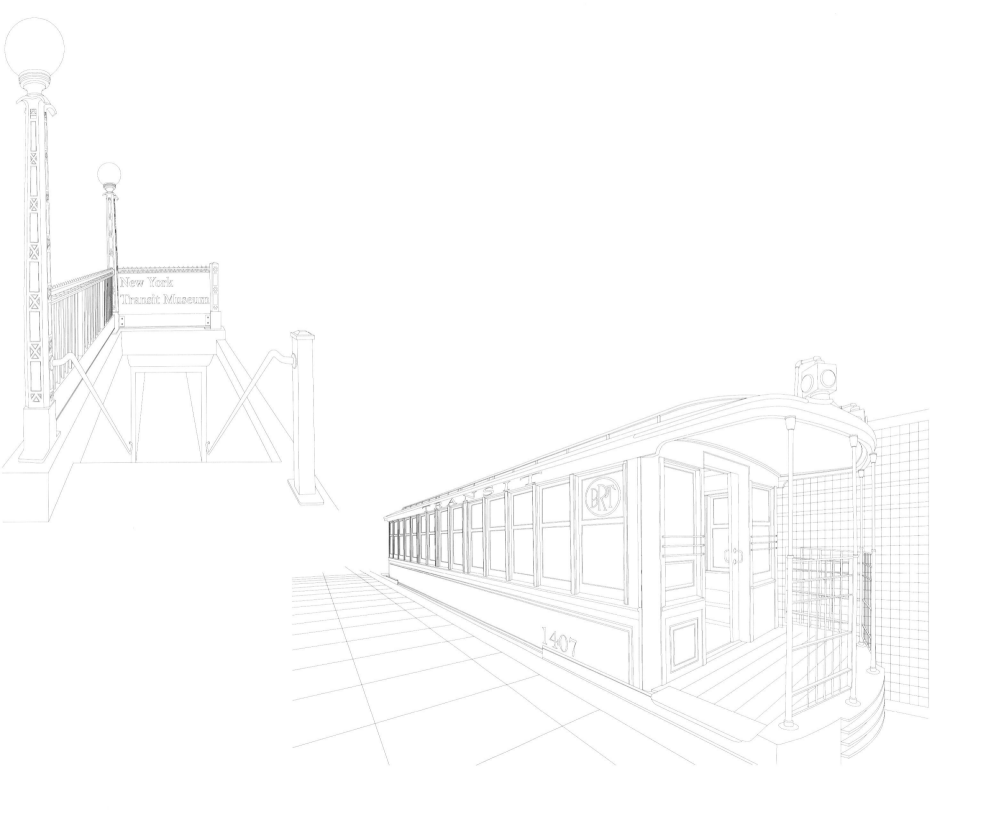

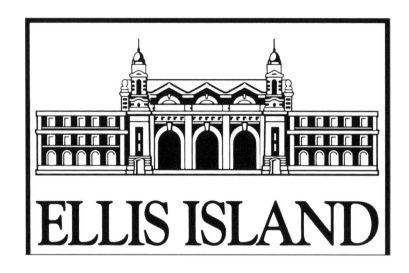

ELLIS ISLAND MUSEUM

Over 12 million immigrants passed through Ellis Island's halls from 1892 to 1954, serving as their gateway to American freedom and opportunity. In 1630, New Amsterdam bought a mud bank in Upper New York Bay, and named it "Oyster Island". Samuel Ellis sold the island to New York State in 1808. The Federal Government then bought Ellis Island and opened a Federal Immigration Station there in 1892. In World War I, German sympathizers were held at Ellis Island. The 1921 Quota Law and 1924 Immigration Act limited the flow of immigrants, making Ellis Island a detention station. During World War II, the island held 7000 German, Italian, and Japanese citizens. In 1950, 1500 Communists and Fascists were held at Ellis Island. In 1954, Ellis Island was placed under the General Services Administration. In 1965, President Lyndon Johnson's Proclamation 3656 added Ellis Island to the Statue of Liberty Monument and under the National Parks Service's care. In 1976, Ellis Island reopened, and added an Immigration Museum in 1990.

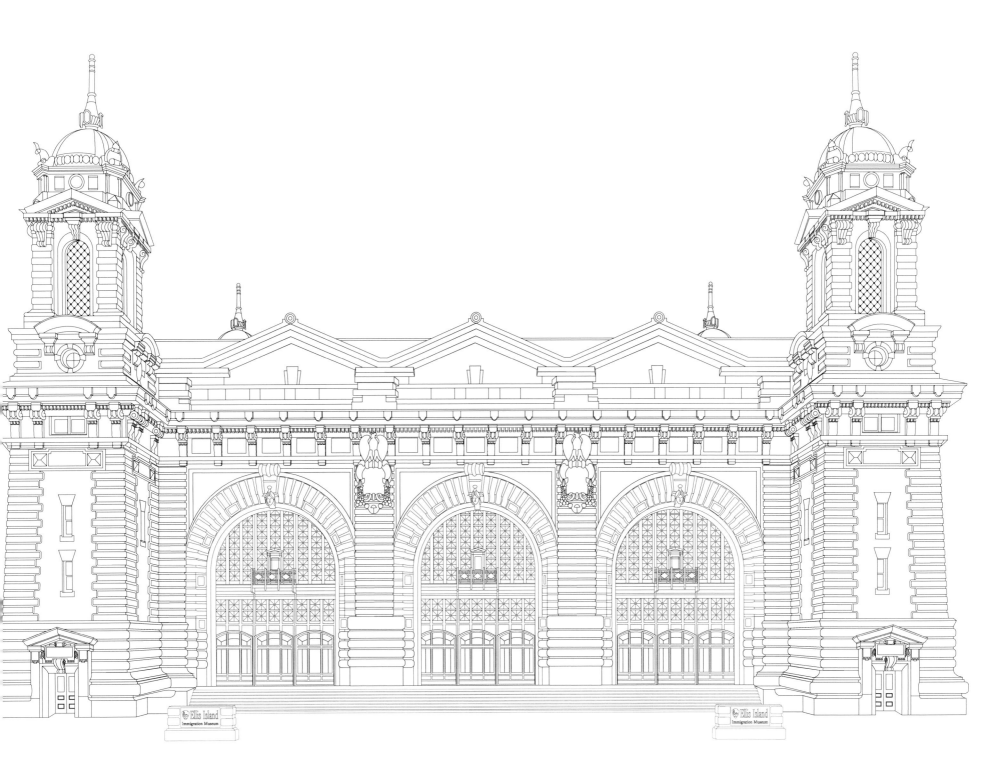

Having recently graduated with a degree in history, Jake Rose pursues his passion for architecture, photography, and most importantly, historic landmarks.

As a long-time resident and major fan of this fascinating city, Jake honors its unique historical institutions in his signature style. Collaborating with artists around the world, beautiful line drawings are created using Jake's own photographs, which are each accompanied by a rich detailed history which makes it unique in the world of coloring books.

The seventh edition in the "Color Our Town" series, "Color NYC Museums" celebrates the multitude of the city's most breathtaking museums.